INVISIBLE SCARS

Lily Hawthorne

Copyright © 2024 Lily Hawthorne

<u>Dedication</u>

"The strongest people are not those who show strength in front of us, but those who fight their battles behind closed doors." – Lily Hawthorne

Dedicated to all those who fight unseen battles.

TABLE OF CONTENTS

Chapter 1

MY JOURNEY: A SPARK FOR HOPE

"No one can make you feel inferior without your consent." -
Eleanor Roosevelt

These words of Eleanor Roosevelt resonate deeply with me now, but there was a time when I had unwittingly given my consent, allowing my self-worth to be whittled away by the narcissist in my life.

Before diving into the complexities of narcissistic abuse, I want to share a piece of my own story. This isn't just a textbook issue for me; it's a lived experience, one that left invisible scars but ultimately fueled the fire of my recovery.

For years, I was entangled in a relationship with a narcissist. In the beginning, it felt like a fairytale romance. He showered me with affection and made me feel like the centre of his universe. I was drawn in by his charisma, his grand gestures, his seeming adoration of me. Little did I know, this was just the first phase of the narcissistic cycle - the idealisation stage. Looking back, there were red flags from the start. He would subtly put me down, comparing me unfavourably to his exes or making "jokes" at my expense. But I brushed it off, convinced it was just his sense of humour. When he started to control who I spent time with and monopolise my attention, I told myself it was because he loved me so much. Slowly but surely, the cracks began to show. The idealisation phase gave way to devaluation. The loving words turned into constant criticism. He possessed an unshakable confidence in his views. Challenging him felt fultile, so, I'd simply agree and withdraw.

The manipulation was insidious. He would twist my words, making me doubt my perceptions. If I tried to express my feelings, he would shut me down, telling me I was being too sensitive or irrational. He had a way of making everything about him, centring himself as the victim in every situation. I felt myself shrinking, losing touch with who I was. It was frustrating. Friends and family couldn't see past his popularity, leaving me feeling unheard and isolated.

Looking back, I realise I was naive when I got married at the age of twenty-one. I was filled with the joy and excitement of starting a new chapter in my life. I envisioned a future filled with love, children, and a happy home. Unfortunately, it soon became clear that I had married a narcissist. I didn't realise it at the time, but I now understand that I had followed a path of familiar torture, as I had been brought up alongside a master manipulator. At that stage, their behaviour had been normalised for me, so I couldn't see it.

Initially, I was showered with affection, attention, and praise. I felt special and loved. This idealisation stage was intoxicating; I believed I had found my soulmate. However, as our relationship progressed, the compliments turned into criticism. I was regularly put down, I felt unheard and his gaslighting made me question my own perceptions. I felt increasingly confused, insecure, and isolated.

I had no financial independence or decision-making abilities. I was taking 'cast-off clothing' from friends and family as I had no funds of my own. My monthly allowance covered my car payments, insurance, food shopping, and clothes for the children. It was almost impossible to have enough petrol left for the car, never mind a night out with my friends or even a trip to the hairdresser. Meanwhile, my husband drove around in sports cars, wheeling and dealing at work and enjoying regular nights out with his mates.

His behaviour became worse; he would often go out with his friends, coming home in the early hours 'worse for wear.' After one particularly boozy night, I remember him lifting our baby from his little cot in the early hours of the morning and then laying him down at the end of our bed. I was too terrified to move in case my 10-week-old baby son fell to the floor. He picked the baby up again after a few minutes, thinking it was funny and telling me I was overreacting. 'It was a joke,' apparently. He once threw a £20 note at me to change a nappy as he was too hungover to do it himself. This demeaning behaviour just increasingly got worse over time.

I became dependent on him, craving the glimpses of affection he would occasionally toss my way. The cycle of idealisation and devaluation kept me tethered, always hoping things would go back to how they were in the beginning. The gaslighting was the worst part. He would blatantly lie, then deny ever saying certain things. I started to question my sanity, wondering if I was losing my grip on reality. The self-doubt was crippling.

Despite our differences, I stayed for the sake of our young children. Leaving wasn't an option back then, but eventually things changed. Outsiders couldn't understand why I stayed, and truthfully, neither could I. I just knew I was drowning, and I couldn't find my way to the surface.

It wasn't until a close friend gently pointed out the signs of abuse that things started to shift. She shared resources with me stories of others who had been through similar experiences. Slowly, the fog began to lift. I started to recognise the patterns, to put a name to what I had been enduring: narcissistic abuse. Equipped with this knowledge, I began to fortify myself. I sought therapy, surrounding myself with a supportive network. I started to reconnect with my sense of self, rediscovering the parts of me I had lost in the relationship. It wasn't an easy road - healing rarely is - but each step brought me closer to reclaiming my power.

The turning point came when I finally walked away for good. Leaving the children's father was an agonising choice, but their well-being came first. His behaviour wasn't healthy for them, and I knew I had to protect them.

Maintaining some contact for the children's sake was inevitable, but I was determined to navigate it in a way that kept them safe. I knew I needed to learn new strategies to safeguard myself and the children from his negativity.

His attempts to manipulate the situation, portraying himself as the victim and diminishing my worth to everyone who would listen, were hurtful. However, I wouldn't let it deter me. My focus was to build a safe and supportive environment for our children.

I started to see my worth and understand that the abuse was never my fault. I mourned the loss of the relationship I thought I had, but I also celebrated the rebirth of my own identity. I was no longer a shell of myself, living to please a narcissist. I was me again, scars and all.

The happy ending to this chapter of my life is that after that relationship ended, I met and married my soulmate. I have been happily married to a kind, considerate, and loving man who has shown me what a healthy, supportive relationship looks like. While the scars of my past will always be a part of me, they no longer define me. I have learned, grown, and healed in ways I never thought possible.

As I reflect on my journey, I'm reminded of a quote by Dwayne Johnson: "I found that with depression, one of the most important things you could realise is that you're not alone." This sentiment rings true for narcissistic abuse as well. In the thick of it, the isolation can be all-consuming. But the truth is, there is a whole community of survivors out there. We may have walked different paths, but our destination is the same - healing, empowerment, and a life free from abuse. My story is not unique, but it is my own. And in sharing it, I hope to offer a spark of hope to others who may be struggling. Narcissistic abuse is an insidious beast, one that can make you question your reality and lose sight of who you are. But I'm here to tell you that recovery is possible. The scars may never fully fade, but they can serve as a reminder of your strength and resilience.

In the chapters to come, we'll dive deeper into the dynamics of narcissistic abuse, exploring the tactics, the effects, and the path to healing. We'll dissect the narcissistic personality, learning to spot the red flags and protect ourselves from future abuses. And most importantly, we'll focus on reclaiming our power, our identities, and our lives.

This journey is not an easy one, but it is a necessary one. As Marcus Aurelius reminds us, "Living a good life is about the potential you possess. You have to learn the art of indifference. Focus on what truly matters, and let the rest become background static. Your indifference is your shield." In the context of narcissistic abuse, this means learning to detach from the narcissist's manipulation to focus on our healing and growth. It's a process of unlearning the lies we've been told and relearning our truth. It's about rediscovering our voices, our boundaries, and our self-worth. It's a journey of shedding the invisible scars and stepping into the light of our own power.

If you're reading this, know that you are not alone. Your experiences are valid, your pain is real, and your healing is possible. You may feel broken, but I promise you, there is a strength within you that cannot be shattered. The fact that you're here, seeking understanding and support, is a testament to your resilience. So, take a deep breath. Acknowledge the courage it takes to confront this issue head-on. And know that with each page turned, you're taking a step towards your own liberation. The road ahead may be rocky at times, but it leads to a place of genuine peace, self-love, and unshakable strength.

In sharing my story, I offer you a hand to hold on this journey. Let my words be a reminder that the darkness does not last forever. There is a light within you that no narcissist can extinguish. And together, we will learn to not only survive but thrive in the aftermath of narcissistic abuse.

As we embark on this path of understanding and overcoming, let us carry with us the wisdom of those who have walked before us. Let us remember Maya Angelou's powerful words: "I can be changed by what happens to me. But I refuse to be reduced by it." Narcissistic abuse may have shaped our experiences, but it does not define our identity. We are not the sum of our scars. We are the embodiment of our resilience, our growth, and our unbreakable spirits.

So, let us move forward with courage, with compassion for ourselves and others, and with a commitment to our own healing. The journey ahead may not be easy, but it is worth every step. Together, we will turn our invisible scars into badges of strength, our pain into purpose, and our experiences into a guiding light for others.

Welcome to the path of healing. May you find solace, support, and empowerment in these pages. May you always remember you are not alone, you are not to blame, and you are worthy of love and respect.

With each of you in my heart, let us step into the light and begin.

Chapter 2

BREAKING FREE AND SHARING THE PATH

"You must be the change you wish to see in the world." -

Mahatma Gandhi

These words of Mahatma Gandhi took on new meaning for me as I embarked on my healing journey from narcissistic abuse. I realised that my recovery wasn't just about my own well-being; it was about lighting the way for others who were still trapped in the darkness.

The journey to healing wasn't easy, but it was undeniably empowering. As I learned to identify the narcissist's tactics and understand the dynamics of abuse, I began to reclaim my power. The invisible scars started fading as I rediscovered my inner strength and self-compassion.

One of the first steps in my healing was education. I devoured every resource I could find on narcissistic personality disorder and the cycle of abuse. Knowledge truly was power - the more I understood, the less hold the narcissist had over me. I learned about gaslighting, love bombing, and the insidious ways a narcissist could twist reality. Seeing these tactics laid out so clearly was like a fog lifting from my mind. I also learned the importance of setting boundaries. For so long, I had allowed the narcissist to trample over my needs, my wants, my very identity. Rebuilding my boundaries was a process of relearning my own values. I started small, saying no to requests that made me uncomfortable asserting my opinions even when they differed from the narcissist's. Each boundary set was a reclamation of my power, a step towards breaking free from the narcissist's control.

Therapy was a crucial component of my healing. Having a safe space to process my experiences and validate my emotions was transformative. My therapist helped me untangle the web of manipulation and see the abuse for what it was. She guided me through the grief of losing the relationship I thought I had and the anger at the injustice of it all. Most importantly, she helped me rebuild my self-worth to see that the abuse was never my fault.

Support groups were another lifeline. Connecting with other survivors and hearing their stories was a powerful reminder that I wasn't alone. We shared coping strategies, celebrated each other's victories, and held space for the harder moments. These connections were a balm to the isolation I had felt for so long. They were proof that healing was possible, that there was life after narcissistic abuse.

As I progressed in my own recovery, I felt a growing need to share what I had learned. I started small, sharing articles and resources with friends who confided in me about their own toxic relationships.

One of the most profound realisations in my healing was that forgiveness was not a requirement. For so long, I had been pressured to forgive the narcissist, to let go of my anger and hurt. But I came to understand that forgiveness was a personal choice, not an obligation. I could release the hold the narcissist had on me without excusing their actions. I could move forward without offering absolution.

Instead, I focused on self-forgiveness. I had to forgive myself for staying as long as I did and for not seeing the abuse sooner. I had to forgive myself for the times I doubted my own perceptions, for the moments I believed the narcissist's lies. This self-forgiveness was a balm to my soul, a recognition that I had done the best I could with what I knew at the time. As I continued to heal and grow, I began to reimagine my life. For so long, the narcissist had been at the centre of my world, dictating my every move. Now, I had the freedom to create a life on my own terms. I rediscovered hobbies I had let fall by the wayside; I nurtured friendships that had been neglected. I learned to prioritise my own needs and to listen to my own voice.

This reimagining wasn't without its challenges. There were times the old doubts would creep in, the echoes of the narcissist's voice in my head. But I had a toolbox now, filled with self-care practices, grounding techniques, and a support network to lean on. I was no longer at the mercy of the narcissist's manipulation. Healing from narcissistic abuse is not a linear process. There were setbacks, moments where I felt I had taken two steps forward and one step back. But even in those harder times, I could see how far I had come. I was no longer the shell of a person; I had been in the throes of abuse. I was stronger, wiser, and more committed to my own well-being.

Looking back, I see that my journey was not just about surviving narcissistic abuse; it was about learning to thrive in its aftermath. It was about reclaiming my identity, my power, and my joy. It was about discovering that I was capable of so much more than I ever believed possible. And now, I turn my attention to you, dear reader. If you find yourself resonating with these words, please know that you are not alone. The path to healing may feel daunting, but it is a path well-trodden by those who have come before you. There is a community waiting to embrace you, to support you, to remind you of your inherent worth. Your healing may not look like mine, and that's okay. We each have our own unique journey to navigate. But there are some universal truths that I hope you will carry with you. You are not to blame for the abuse you endured. You are worthy of love, respect, and compassion.

And most importantly, you have the power within you to break free and create a life of your own design. It takes courage to confront the pain of narcissistic abuse, to face the invisible scars left behind. But know that with each step, you are moving towards the light. Each boundary set, each moment of self-compassion, each reach for support - these are all acts of profound bravery.

Remember, healing is not about perfection. It's about progress, about learning to extend grace to ourselves on the harder days and celebrate the victories, no matter how small. It's about unlearning the lies the narcissist taught us and relearning our own inherent truth.

Some days, the healing may feel like a battle, an uphill climb against the residue of trauma. On those days, I invite you to lean on the words of the poet Rupi Kaur: "I am not a victim. I am a survivor. I not only survived, but I thrived. I not only thrived, I conquered." Let these words be a mantra, a reminder of your unbreakable spirit.

As you navigate this path, know that you have a right to your anger, your grief, and your full spectrum of emotions. Healing is not about suppressing these feelings but rather learning to process them in a healthy way. Lean on your support system, whether that's a therapist, a trusted friend, or a support group. Allow yourself to feel, to cry, to rage when needed. These emotions are not a sign of weakness; they are a testament to your strength. And on the days when hope feels distant when the shadows of the past feel all-consuming, I invite you to return to these pages. Let the stories shared here be a reminder that hope is always on the horizon. You are part of a community of survivors, each lighting the way for the next. Your story, your healing, is a beacon of hope for someone still trapped in the darkness.

So, dear reader, I end this chapter with a call to action. Continue to educate yourself, seek support, and prioritise your own healing. But also, when you feel ready, consider sharing your own story. Your voice has power, and your experiences matter. You never know who might need to hear your words, who might find solace and strength in knowing they're not alone. Together, we can break the silence around narcissistic abuse. We can create a world where survivors are believed, supported, and empowered. We can turn our collective pain into a force for change, for healing, for hope. The road ahead may be challenging, but it is also filled with possibilities. With each step, you are reclaiming your power, your identity, and your life. As you walk this path, know that you are surrounded by a community of survivors, cheering you on every step of the way. You are resilient. You are worthy. You are a survivor. And together, we will continue to turn our invisible scars into triumphs, our pain into purpose, and our experiences into a guiding light for others.

So, keep going, your healing is a journey, and every step counts. Trust in your own strength, lean on your support, and remember that you are never alone. The light within you is inextinguishable, and it will guide you home to yourself.

With each of you in my heart, I invite you to turn the page and continue on this path of healing, one brave step at a time. Together, we rise.

Chapter 3

WHY IT ALL MATTERS

"Give every day the chance to become the most beautiful day of your life." Mark Twain

---

ark Twain's words resonate deeply with me, especially in light of my journey through and out of narcissistic abuse. In the depths of that dark period, I couldn't imagine a beautiful day, let alone a beautiful life. But here I am, not just surviving but thriving, and it's because I've learned to give each day that chance.

My story is not unique. Millions of people worldwide face the challenges of narcissistic abuse. I'm sharing my experiences, my insights, and my heart in these pages for you if you suspect you're in a similar situation or if you're struggling with the aftermath of a narcissistic relationship. Consider this a beacon of hope, a guide to understanding the complexities of this insidious form of abuse, and ultimately, a roadmap to healing.

When I was in the throes of narcissistic abuse, I felt utterly alone. The manipulation, the gaslighting, the constant erosion of my sense of self - it was a heavy burden to bear, made heavier by the isolation. I didn't understand what was happening to me. I doubted my own perceptions and questioned my own sanity. If you're in a similar place right now, I want you to know that you're not alone, and it's not your fault.

Narcissistic abuse is a sinister dance, one where the steps are constantly changing, and the rules are never in your favour. Narcissists are master manipulators skilled at twisting reality and making you doubt yourself. They chip away at your self-esteem, isolate you from your support systems, and leave you feeling like a shell of your former self. It's a gradual process, one that can be hard to recognise when you're in the midst of it. That's why I'm sharing my story because I know firsthand how validating it can be to see your experiences reflected in someone else's words. When I first started learning about narcissistic abuse, it was like a lightbulb went off. Suddenly, I had a name for what I was experiencing. I wasn't crazy, I wasn't oversensitive, I wasn't the problem. It was a revelation that changed the course of my life.

In the pages to come, I'll be diving deep into the dynamics of narcissistic abuse. We'll explore the traits of narcissistic personality disorder, the cycle of abuse, and the insidious tactics narcissists use to control and manipulate their victims. But more than that, wc'll bc shining a light on the path to healing. Because here's the truth: healing is possible. It's not easy, and it's not quick, but it is absolutely achievable. I know because I've lived it. When I first left my narcissistic relationship, I was a wreck. I was dealing with complex PTSD, struggling with self-doubt and self-blame, and felt utterly lost. But little by little, day by day, I started to reclaim myself. It started with educating myself, learning everything I could about narcissistic abuse. Knowledge is power, and understanding what I'd been through was the first step in liberating myself from shame and self-blame. I devoured books, articles, and online resources. I connected with other survivors, finding solace and strength in their stories.

Therapy was a game-changer for me. Having a safe space to process my experiences, validate my emotions, and learn coping strategies was integral to my healing. If you're able, I can't recommend seeking professional help enough. A skilled therapist can be an invaluable ally on your healing journey. Narcissists are notorious for violating boundaries, for pushing and pushing until they get their way. Part of my healing was learning to say no, to put my own needs first, and to stick to my boundaries even in the face of manipulation and pushback. Self-care became non-negotiable. I had to relearn how to nurture myself and how to treat myself with kindness and compassion. This looked like daily practices of meditation, journaling, and movement. It looked like I surrounded myself with positive, supportive people. It looked like allowing myself to feel my emotions, to grieve, to rage, to heal. One of the most profound shifts came when I started focusing on my personal growth. For so long, my entire identity had been wrapped up in my relationship. I had lost sight of who I was, of what I wanted, of what brought me joy. Rediscovering myself was a journey of trial and error, exploring new hobbies, and revisiting old passions. It was a process of reconnecting with my inner wisdom, of learning to trust myself again.

As I healed, I found my voice. I started speaking out about my experiences, first in support groups, then to friends and family. The more I shared, the more I realised how many others had stories just like mine. Breaking the silence around narcissistic abuse became a passion, a purpose. That's why I'm writing these words now, why I'm pouring my heart onto these pages. Because I know the power of a story, the impact of seeing your pain reflected in someone else's journey. If my words can offer hope to even one person, if they can light the way for someone else's healing, then every bit of my struggle will have been worth it. But this isn't just about my story. Throughout these chapters, you'll find the insights and expertise of professionals in the field of narcissistic abuse recovery. You'll learn about the psychological impacts of long-term emotional abuse and proven strategies for healing. You'll find exercises and prompts to help you process your own experiences and move forward in your journey. More than anything, you'll find empathy, validation, and understanding because one of the most insidious aspects of narcissistic abuse is how it makes you question your reality. Narcissists are adept at gaslighting, at making you doubt your own perceptions and experiences. By sharing my story and the stories of others, I hope to offer a counterpoint to show you that your experiences are real, they're valid, and they matter.

If you're currently in a relationship with a narcissist, this can be your lifeline. It's the resource I wish I had when I was in the depths of confusion and pain, wondering if I was losing my mind. These pages will help you recognise the patterns of abuse, understand the tactics narcissists use, and start to formulate a plan for your own safety and well-being. If you've already left a narcissistic relationship, consider this your companion on the road to recovery. Healing from narcissistic abuse is a process, one that often involves complex PTSD, anxiety, depression, and a host of other challenges. The stories and strategies shared here will validate your experiences, offer practical tools for coping and healing, and remind you that you're not alone. And if you're a supporter of someone who's experienced narcissistic abuse, these words can help you understand what your loved one is going through. Narcissistic abuse is a complex trauma, one that's often misunderstood by those on the outside. By educating yourself, you'll be better equipped to offer empathy, support, and understanding of your loved one's needs.

Ultimately, this is a book about hope. It's a testament to the resilience of the human spirit, to our innate capacity to heal and thrive even after unimaginable pain. It's a reminder that no matter how dark things seem, there is always light ahead. As I reflect on my own journey, I'm astounded by how far I've come. From the shell of a person I was to the firm, resilient, joyful woman I am today, the transformation has been nothing short of miraculous. And I want you to know that the same transformation is possible for you. No matter where you are in your journey, know that you have the strength within you to overcome this. You have the wisdom, the resilience, and the courage to reclaim your life. It won't be easy, and it won't happen overnight, but it is possible. And you don't have to do it alone. There is a whole community of survivors out here, ready to support you, validate you, and cheer you on. Reach out, share your story, and let yourself be seen and heard. There is immense power in breaking the silence, in refusing to let shame and secrecy win.

This is your invitation to step into your own healing, to give yourself the chance to create the beautiful life you deserve. It's an invitation to join a revolution of survivors, each reclaiming their power and rewriting their stories.

In the pages to come, we'll be walking this path together. We'll be diving into the complexities of narcissistic abuse, yes, but more importantly, we'll be focusing on the triumph of healing. We'll be celebrating the strength and resilience of survivors and offering tangible tools and strategies for reclaiming your life.

So, take a deep breath and know that you're exactly where you need to be. Whether you're just starting to recognise the patterns of abuse in your relationship, you're in the midst of leaving, or you're well on your way to recovery, this is your sign to keep going. Keep fighting. Keep believing in yourself and your worth.

You are not alone. You are not to blame. You are worthy of love, respect, and joy. And you have the power within you to create the life you deserve.

Let's turn the page together and step into the beautiful journey of healing ahead. Your story is just beginning.

Chapter 4

SHINING A LIGHT ON NARCISSISTIC ABUSE

"The best revenge is not to be like your enemy." Marcus Aurelius

These wise words from Marcus Aurelius have been a guiding light for me on my healing journey from narcissistic abuse. In the depths of my pain, I was tempted to lash out, to fight fire with fire, to become as manipulative and hurtful as my abuser. But I realised that true power, true healing, comes from rising above, from refusing to let their tactics define me.

Now, let's delve deeper into understanding narcissistic abuse. When I first started learning about Narcissistic Personality Disorder (NPD), it was like a lightbulb went off in my mind. NPD is a mental health condition characterised by an inflated sense of self-importance, a deep need for excessive attention and admiration, and a lack of empathy for others. People with this disorder often believe they are superior to others and have little regard for other people's feelings. But here's the thing: understanding the clinical definition of NPD is just the tip of the iceberg when it comes to unravelling the complexities of narcissistic abuse. It's one thing to read about the traits of a narcissist on paper; it's another entirely to experience them firsthand in a relationship.

Narcissistic abuse is a form of emotional abuse where the abuser uses manipulation, gaslighting, and control to maintain power over their victim. It's a gradual, insidious process that can be hard to recognise when you're in the midst of it. Narcissists are master manipulators skilled at twisting reality and making you doubt your perceptions.

One of the critical traits of a narcissist is their grandiose sense of self-importance. They believe they are special and unique and can only be understood by or should associate with other special or high-status people or institutions. This grandiosity is often coupled with a deep need for admiration. Narcissists crave constant validation and attention, often going to extreme lengths to receive it.

But beneath this grandiose exterior often lies a fragile self-esteem. Narcissists can be incredibly sensitive to criticism or defeat and can react with rage or contempt when they feel threatened. This is where the abuse often escalates. When a narcissist feels their power slipping, they'll often double down on their manipulative tactics to regain control.

Gaslighting is a common tactic employed by narcissists. It's a form of psychological manipulation where the abuser seeks to sow seeds of doubt in the victim's mind, making them question their own memory, perception, and sanity. They might blatantly lie, deny things they've said or done, or twist your words to fit their narrative. Over time, this constant questioning of your reality can lead to extreme self-doubt and confusion.

Narcissists are also skilled at emotional manipulation. They might use love bombing - overwhelming you with affection and attention in the early stages of the relationship - only to withdraw that affection abruptly as a form of punishment. They might play on your insecurities, using your deepest fears and vulnerabilities against you. They might regularly invalidate your emotions, telling you that you're overreacting or too sensitive when you express hurt or frustration.

Another tactic is isolation. Narcissists often seek to isolate their victims from friends, family, and any other support systems. They might discourage you from seeing certain people or create drama when you do. They might demand all of your time and attention, leaving little room for anyone else. This isolation makes it harder for you to get outside perspectives and easier for the narcissist to control the narrative.

Control is at the heart of narcissistic abuse. Narcissists have an insatiable need for control, both over their own lives and the lives of those around them. They might try to control your every move, from what you wear to who you talk to. They might use financial abuse, controlling all the money and making you account for every penny. They might use threats, intimidation, or even physical violence to maintain their control.

Living under this constant barrage of manipulation, gaslighting, and control can have devastating effects on your mental and emotional health. You might start to question your own reality, constantly second-guessing yourself. You might blame yourself for the abuse, thinking if you could just be better, do better, and be more understanding, the abuse would stop. You might develop complex PTSD, anxiety, depression, and a host of other mental health challenges.

But here's what I want you to know: the abuse is not your fault. No matter what the narcissist says, no matter how they try to twist reality, you are not to blame for their actions. Narcissistic abuse is about power and control, not love. It's not about you being good enough; it's about them maintaining their grip on power. Recognising the patterns of abuse is the first step to reclaiming your power. When you can name the tactics and see the manipulation for what it is, it starts to lose its hold over you. It's like turning on a light in a dark room - suddenly, you can see the outlines of the furniture, the exit door. You're no longer stumbling around in the dark.

Education is key. The more you learn about narcissistic abuse, the more equipped you'll be to recognise it and resist it. Read books, articles, and online resources. Connect with other survivors who understand what you're going through. Seek out the guidance of a therapist who specialises in narcissistic abuse recovery.

Start to set boundaries. Narcissists thrive on violating boundaries and pushing until they get their way. Learning to set and maintain firm boundaries is crucial to your healing. This might mean learning to say no, even in the face of pushback. It might mean limiting contact with the narcissist or cutting them out of your life entirely. It's not easy, but it's necessary for your well-being.

Prioritise self-care. Narcissistic abuse can leave you feeling drained, depleted, and disconnected from yourself. Rediscovering self-care is an act of resistance, a way of reclaiming your power. This might look like daily practices of meditation, journaling, or movement. It might mean surrounding yourself with positive, supportive people. It might mean allowing yourself to feel your emotions, to grieve, to rage, to heal.

Focus on your own personal growth. Narcissistic relationships can stunt your growth, making you doubt your own abilities and passions. Part of healing is rediscovering who you are outside of the relationship. Explore new hobbies and revisit old interests. Connect with your own inner wisdom and your sense of purpose. As you grow and thrive, the narcissist's grip on you will start to loosen.

Find your voice. Narcissistic abuse thrives in silence and secrecy. Speaking your truth and sharing your story are powerful acts of defiance. It's a way of saying, "I will not be silenced. My experiences matter." Whether it's in a support group, with trusted friends and family, or through your own creative expression, finding your voice is integral to healing.

Build a support network. Surround yourself with people who see you, believe you, and support you unconditionally. This might include friends, family, a therapist, or a support group of fellow survivors. Having a solid support system can counteract the isolation and self-doubt that narcissistic abuse breeds.

Practice self-compassion. Healing from narcissistic abuse is a journey, and it's not always a linear one. There will be good days and bad days, steps forward and steps back. Be gentle with yourself. Treat yourself with the same kindness and understanding you would extend to a dear friend. Remember that healing is a process, and your worth is not contingent on your progress.

Hold onto hope. When you're in the thick of narcissistic abuse, hope can feel like a distant light flickering on the horizon. But I promise you, there is hope. There is life after narcissistic abuse, and it's a life filled with freedom, joy, and self-love. Keep putting one foot in front of the other; keep reaching for that light. You will get there.

As I reflect on my own journey of healing, I'm reminded of the incredible strength and resilience of the human spirit. Those of us who have endured narcissistic abuse have been through the fire, and we have emerged on the other side, scarred but not broken. We have faced the darkest parts of human nature, and we have chosen to keep our own light shining.

Your scars, invisible as they may be, are a testament to your survival. They are proof of your courage, your resilience, and your unbreakable spirit. Wear them with pride, for they are badges of honour in a battle most will never understand. As you continue on your healing journey, remember that you are not alone. There is a community of survivors standing with you, cheering you on, holding space for your healing. Together, we are breaking the silence around narcissistic abuse. Together, we are reclaiming our power, our voices, and our lives. Together, we can turn those invisible scars into a testament to our resilience, a beacon of hope for those still in the darkness. Together, we can create a world where love doesn't hurt, where abuse is never tolerated, and where every individual is free to thrive.

It won't be easy, and it won't happen overnight. Healing is a journey, and it's a journey that requires incredible courage and commitment. But I promise you, it's a journey worth taking. Because on the other side of that journey is a life of freedom, authenticity, and unshakable self-worth.

So, keep going. Keep shining your light. Keep believing in your own strength and resilience. And most of all, keep holding onto hope. For hope is the light that guides us out of the darkness, the hand that reaches out to pull us up when we've fallen, the voice that whispers, "Keep going. You've got this." With every step you take, you are not just healing yourself; you are paving the way for others. Your survival, your resilience, your willingness to keep going - it's a powerful inspiration to those who are still finding their way.

In the words of Maya Angelou, *"I can be changed by what happens to me. But I refuse to be reduced by it."* Let this be your mantra, your rallying cry. Yes, narcissistic abuse may have changed you. It may have left scars, visible and invisible. But it does not define you. It does not reduce your worth, your potential, or your inherent beauty. You are so much more than what happened to you. You are a survivor, a thriver, a force to be reckoned with. And your story, your healing, your triumph - it matters. It matters more than you could know.

So, keep turning the pages of your story, and keep writing the chapters of your healing. And trust that with every page turned, you are getting closer to the life you deserve - a life of peace, empowerment, and unshakable self-love. Together, we rise. Together, we heal. Together, we reclaim our power and rewrite our stories. And together, we create a world where love always triumphs over abuse, where light always conquers darkness, and where every individual is free to shine their brightest light.

Keep shining. The world needs your light.

Chapter 5

THE TWO FACES OF NARCISSISM

"The only thing necessary for the triumph of evil is for good men to do nothing." - Edmund Burke

These profound words from Edmund Burke echo in my mind as I delve deeper into the complex world of narcissistic abuse. For far too long, the insidious nature of narcissism has been allowed to thrive in the shadows, unchecked and unchallenged. But as survivors, as "good men" and women, we have the power to shine a light on this evil, to expose its many faces, and to triumph over its destructive force.

In the realm of narcissism, two distinct types emerge: grandiose and vulnerable. While both stem from the same core of narcissistic personality disorder, they manifest in strikingly different ways. Understanding these two faces of narcissism is crucial in recognising the signs of abuse and in navigating the complex dynamics of a narcissistic relationship.

Let's start with grandiose narcissism, the face that is perhaps most familiar in the public perception of narcissism. Those with grandiose narcissistic traits often present an image of supreme confidence, even arrogance. They exude an air of superiority, believing themselves to be above the rules and constraints that govern the rest of us, mere mortals. This grandiosity often has its roots in childhood. Many individuals with grandiose narcissistic traits were likely treated as superior or above others during their formative years. Perhaps they were constantly praised for their talents, their looks, and their intelligence, to the point where they internalised this sense of being extraordinary. Or maybe they were given special treatment, allowed to bend the rules and escape consequences, reinforcing the notion that they were above the norm. As they move into adulthood, these childhood experiences shape their interactions with the world. Grandiose narcissists often have a deep need for admiration and validation. They crave the spotlight and will go to great lengths to ensure they remain the centre of attention. This can manifest in constant bragging, name-dropping, or self-aggrandisement. They may regale you with tales of their achievements, their connections, their superior taste or intellect.

There's an elitism to grandiose narcissism, a belief that they are part of a special class or tier of society. They may look down on others, seeing them as inferior or beneath their notice. This can lead to a profound lack of empathy as they struggle to see beyond their own needs and desires. In interpersonal relationships, grandiose narcissists can be deeply charming... at first. They often excel at first impressions, sweeping you off your feet with their charisma and grand gestures. But as the relationship progresses, their true colours begin to show. They may become increasingly demanding of your time and attention, expecting you to prioritise them above all else. They may react with rage or contempt if they feel slighted or if their fragile ego is bruised.

Control is a crucial theme with grandiose narcissists. They have an insatiable need for control over their environment and the people in it. This can manifest in overt ways, such as dictating how you dress or who you socialise with. But it can also take more subtle forms, like monopolising conversations, always needing to have the last word, or making unilateral decisions without considering your input.

Grandiose narcissists are often highly sensitive to criticism. Despite their outward bravado, their self-esteem is actually quite fragile. Any perceived slight or critique can be met with explosive anger or cold, silent treatments. They may lash out in an attempt to regain control, belittling or intimidating their critic into submission.

In the face of this aggression, it's easy to feel powerless. Grandiose narcissists have a way of making you question your own reality and your own worth. Their confidence can be mistaken for competence, their arrogance for actual superiority. But it's crucial to remember that their behaviour is not about you - it's about their own deep-seated insecurities and needs for control.

Recognising the signs of grandiose narcissism is the first step in protecting yourself from its toxic effects. Some key red flags to watch out for include:

1. An inflated sense of self-importance

2. A constant need for admiration and validation

3. A lack of empathy for others

4. A sense of entitlement and a belief in their own superiority

5. Interpersonally exploitative behaviour

6. Arrogance and haughty behaviours or attitudes

If you find yourself in a relationship with a grandiose narcissist, it's important to set clear boundaries. This can be challenging, as they are likely to push back against any perceived limits to their control. But standing firm in your boundaries, being willing to say "no," and prioritising your own needs are crucial for your well-being.

Seeking support is also key. Grandiose narcissists are skilled at isolating their partners, making them feel like they are the problem. Reaching out to trusted friends, family, or a therapist can provide a reality check and a support system to lean on.

It's also important to remember that you can't change a grandiose narcissist. No amount of love, patience, or understanding will "fix" them or make them see the error of their ways. The change has to come from within, and most narcissists see no need to change. The best thing you can do is focus on your own healing and growth.

As I reflect on my own experiences with grandiose narcissism, I'm struck by the insidiousness of its impact. When you're in the thick of it, it's easy to lose sight of your own reality, your own sense of self. The constant belittling, the gaslighting, the control - it chips away at you, bit by bit until you hardly recognise yourself. But here's the thing: you are not alone. The very fact that you're here, reading these words, is a testament to your strength and your resilience. You've already taken the first and most important step by acknowledging that something isn't right and seeking to understand the dynamics at play. And understanding is power. The more you learn about narcissistic abuse, the more you'll be able to recognise its signs and protect yourself from its effects. You'll start to see the patterns, the cycles of abuse. You'll begin to reclaim your own narrative, your own truth.

It's not an easy journey, and there will be setbacks along the way. Healing from narcissistic abuse is a process, and it's not always a linear one. There will be days when you doubt yourself, where the old scripts of self-blame and shame creep back in. But with each step forward, each boundary set, each moment of self-compassion, you are reclaiming your power.

One of the most profound realisations in my own journey was understanding that the abuse was never about me. It wasn't about my worth as a person, my lovability, or my value. It was about the narcissist's own deep-seated issues, their own unhealed wounds and insecurities. Realising this was a turning point, a weight lifted from my shoulders.

As you navigate your own healing journey, remember to be gentle with yourself. Recovery is not a race, and there is no finish line. It's a daily practice of choosing yourself, of prioritising your own well-being and growth. Some days will be easier than others, and that's okay. The important thing is that you keep going and keep putting one foot in front of the other. Surround yourself with support, with people who see you and believe in you. Seek out resources and tools that resonate with you, whether that's therapy, support groups, books, or creative outlets. Trust your own inner wisdom and intuition. You know yourself better than anyone else, and you have the answers within you.

Above all, hold onto hope. When you're in the thick of narcissistic abuse, hope can feel like a distant light flickering on the horizon. But I promise you, there is hope.

There is life after narcissistic abuse, and it's a life filled with freedom, joy, and self-love. Keep moving towards that light, even when the path feels dark and treacherous. You will get there. Your story, your journey, is a testament to the incredible resilience of the human spirit. Every day that you choose to keep going, to keep healing, to keep loving yourself - that is a day that the narcissist does not win. That is a day that you reclaim your power and your light. As you step into your own healing, know that you are part of a community of survivors, each on their own journey, each lighting the way for others. Together, we are breaking the silence around narcissistic abuse. Together, we are saying, "no more." Together, we are creating a world where love doesn't hurt, where abuse is never tolerated, and where every individual is free to thrive.

So, keep shining your light. Keep speaking your truth. Keep believing in your own worth and your own power. And know that with every step you take, you are not just healing yourself - you are paving the way for others. You are part of a movement of hope, of healing, of transformation.

The road ahead may be challenging, but it is also filled with incredible possibilities. With each new day, you have the opportunity to write a new story to create a life of your own design. A life filled with genuine love, respect, and joy. A life where your voice is heard, your boundaries are honoured, and your light shines bright. That life is waiting for you. It's calling to you, even now. All you have to do is keep going, keep believing, keep reaching for it. One step at a time, one day at a time, one moment of self-love at a time.

You've got this. And you are never, ever alone.

Keep turning the pages. Your story is just beginning.

Chapter 6

COMPLEXITIES OF VULNERABLE NARCISSISM

> *"The best revenge is to be unlike him who performed the injury."- Marcus Aurelius*

These wise words from Marcus Aurelius have been a guiding light for me on my journey of healing from narcissistic abuse. When faced with the hurt and betrayal inflicted by a narcissist, it's natural to want to lash out, to make them feel the depth of pain they've caused. But in doing so, we risk becoming the very thing we're trying to escape. The true path to healing and freedom lies in focusing on our own growth and refusing to let their dysfunction define us.

In the previous chapter, we explored the grandiose narcissist - the one who presents a confident, often arrogant exterior to the world. But there's another type of narcissism, one that's often harder to spot but no less damaging: vulnerable narcissism.

Vulnerable narcissists, unlike their grandiose counterparts, often come across as shy, sensitive, and even insecure. Their narcissistic traits serve as a defence mechanism, a way to protect themselves from the deep feelings of inadequacy and shame that plague them. Understanding this complex dynamic is crucial in recognising the signs of abuse and in navigating the turbulent waters of a relationship with a vulnerable narcissist. The roots of vulnerable narcissism often lie in childhood trauma. Imagine growing up in an environment where your emotional needs were consistently neglected, where you were criticised, dismissed, or even abused by the very people meant to nurture and protect you. This kind of early trauma can create a deep wound, a pervasive sense of being unworthy and unlovable. As a result, the vulnerable narcissist develops a fragile sense of self, one that requires constant external validation to feel secure. They may present themselves as unique, gifted, or misunderstood, seeking admiration and reassurance to counter their deep-seated feelings of inferiority. They're often susceptible to criticism or perceived slights, their self-esteem rising and falling based on the opinions of others.

This emotional volatility can make relationships with vulnerable narcissists a rollercoaster ride. In the beginning, they may shower you with affection and attention, making you feel like the centre of their world. They can be deeply empathetic and attuned to your needs, creating a strong sense of intimacy and connection. But this idealisation phase is often short-lived. As the relationship progresses, you may find yourself walking on eggshells, never quite sure what will trigger a narcissistic wound. The vulnerable narcissist may become increasingly possessive and demanding, expecting you to be available at their beck and call. They may lash out in anger when they feel slighted, using sarcasm, guilt-tripping, or outright cruelty to regain a sense of control.

Criticism, even when constructive, is often met with extreme defensiveness. The vulnerable narcissist may react with rage, turning the tables to make you feel like you're the one at fault. Or they may withdraw emotionally, retreating into sullen silence as a way to punish and manipulate. This constant push and pull can be deeply destabilising. One moment, you may feel cherished and adored; the next, devalued and discarded. This cycle of idealisation and devaluation is a hallmark of narcissistic abuse, and it can leave you questioning your own reality and self-worth.

Vulnerable narcissists are masters at gaslighting, a form of psychological manipulation in which they sow seeds of doubt in your mind, making you question your own perceptions and memories. They may deny things you know they said, twist your words, or rewrite history to fit their narrative. Over time, this constant erosion of your reality can leave you feeling disoriented, confused, and even crazy.

Another complexity of the vulnerable narcissist is their capacity for empathy. Unlike grandiose narcissists, who often struggle to consider the feelings of others, vulnerable narcissists can be highly attuned to emotional cues. They may even pride themselves on their sensitivity and ability to understand others.

However, this empathy is often selective and self-referential. The vulnerable narcissist may be deeply moved by stories that mirror their own pain but struggle to extend that same compassion to experiences outside their frame of reference. They may use their emotional attunement as a tool for manipulation, to create a sense of intimacy and dependency.

Navigating a relationship with a vulnerable narcissist requires a delicate balance of compassion and firm boundaries. It's important to remember that their hurtful behaviour often stems from a place of deep insecurity and unresolved trauma. Responding with anger or judgment is unlikely to be productive and may only reinforce their negative self-image. At the same time, it's crucial to protect your own emotional well-being. Setting and maintaining clear boundaries is essential, even if it results in narcissistic rage or withdrawal. This may mean learning to assert your needs calmly and firmly, even in the face of manipulation or guilt-tripping. It may mean learning to tolerate the discomfort of disappointing your partner in order to stay true to yourself.

Seeking outside support is also key. The emotional turbulence of a relationship with a vulnerable narcissist can be isolating and confusing. Having a trusted therapist, support group, or network of friends to validate your experiences and provide perspective can be a lifeline. It's also important to maintain a strong sense of self outside the relationship. Vulnerable narcissists often attempt to merge their identity with yours, blurring the lines of individuality. Nurturing your own interests, friendships, and goals can help maintain a healthy sense of autonomy and reduce the impact of narcissistic manipulation.

Ultimately, the decision to stay in or leave a relationship with a vulnerable narcissist is a deeply personal one. For some, the glimpses of the wounded child beneath the narcissistic exterior inspire a desire to help and heal. For others, the emotional toll becomes too high, necessitating a prioritisation of their own well-being. Regardless of your choice, know that healing is possible. The scars of narcissistic abuse, while profound, do not define you. With time, self-compassion, and supportive resources, you can reclaim your sense of self, establish healthy boundaries, and cultivate relationships based on mutual respect and genuine love. One of the most challenging aspects of healing from vulnerable narcissistic abuse is untangling your own sense of reality from the narcissist's distortions. When you've been subjected to constant gaslighting, it can be difficult to trust your own perceptions and instincts. You may second-guess your memories, doubt your emotional responses, and feel a pervasive sense of confusion.

If this resonates with you, know that you are not alone, and you are not to blame. The self-doubt you're experiencing is not a reflection of your own inadequacy but rather a testament to the depth of the manipulation you've endured. Narcissists are skilled at making you question yourself because as long as you're doubting your own reality, you're less likely to challenge theirs.

Reclaiming your truth is a gradual process, one that requires patience and self-compassion. Start by validating your own experiences, even if they contradict the narcissist's narrative. Keep a journal of your interactions and your emotional responses. This can serve as a grounding reference point when the gaslighting fog descends.

Surround yourself with people who see you, believe you, and affirm your reality. Whether it's a therapist, a support group, or trusted loved ones, having a network of validation can be a powerful counterpoint to narcissistic distortion. Practice trusting your gut if something feels off or uncomfortable; honour that instinct. You don't need to justify or rationalise your feelings to anyone, least of all the narcissist. Your discomfort is valid, regardless of how it's received.

Be gentle with yourself as you navigate this process. Unlearning the patterns of narcissistic abuse takes time, and there will be moments of self-doubt and confusion along the way. This is a normal part of the healing journey and does not represent a failure on your part. Every time you choose to honour your own experience, every time you set a boundary or reach out for support, you are taking a stand against the narcissistic distortion. You are reclaiming your narrative, your voice, and your right to your own reality. And as you continue on this path of healing, remember that your worth is intrinsic and unassailable. No amount of narcissistic devaluation can diminish your inherent deservingness of love, respect, and compassion. You are worthy simply because you exist.

Your healing journey is unique to you, and it will unfold in its own perfect timing. Trust your own pace, your own intuition, and your own inner wisdom. You have the strength and the resilience within you to not only survive this experience but to thrive in its aftermath. And as you step into that thriving, know that you are part of a community of survivors, each navigating their own path to healing. Together, we are shattering the silence that allows narcissistic abuse to persist. Together, we are reclaiming our stories and our power. Together, we are building a world where love is nourishing, boundaries are sacred, and every individual's reality is respected.

So, keep walking this path, even when the terrain is rough. Keep reaching out, even when the vulnerability feels daunting. Keep honouring your truth, even when it's met with resistance. Your story matters. Your voice matters. Your healing matters. And with every step forward, you are not only reclaiming your own life - you are lighting the way for others. You are a living testament to the transformative power of healing, to the resilience of the human spirit, and to the unstoppable force of self-love.

Chapter 7

MY JOURNEY: THROUGH THE SHADOWS AND INTO THE LIGHT

"I found that with depression, one of the most important things you could realise is that you're not alone." - Dwayne Johnson

These poignant words from Dwayne Johnson resonate deeply with my own journey, a journey marked by the shadows of narcissistic abuse and the illuminating power of self-discovery and healing.

I grew up in a family of four - Mum, Dad, my older sister Rose, and me. From the outside, we might have appeared to be a typical, loving family. But behind closed doors, a complex dynamic was at play, one that would shape the course of my life in profound ways.

Mum and Dad had an unshakable bond, a love that weathered many storms. But even their strength was tested by the challenges posed by my sister Rose. From an early age, it was clear that Rose was a difficult child. She demanded constant attention, threw tantrums when she didn't get her way, and seemed to delight in creating chaos. My parents, like many of their generation, were at a loss on how to handle her behaviour. They oscillated between giving in to her demands to keep the peace and attempting to set boundaries, which only seemed to fuel her fire.

One of my earliest memories, at the tender age of five, set the stage for the tumultuous relationship I would have with Rose. We were racing to the bathroom, a common occurrence in a household with one toilet, and Rose was determined to win at all costs. She slammed the door shut, and in the process, the top of my index finger was severed. The physical pain was excruciating, but it paled in comparison to the emotional trauma that would follow. As we grew older, Rose's behaviour became more erratic and manipulative. She had a knack for getting what she wanted, no matter the cost. I vividly remember an incident when Rose insisted on getting sweets from the local shop. Mum, in a rare moment of acquiescence, allowed Rose to walk me to the store. What should have been a simple errand turned into a nightmare when we arrived in the middle of an armed robbery. The gunman stood at the entrance, forbidding anyone from entering. But Rose, with a brazenness that made my jaw drop to the floor, confidently told the robber that she wasn't leaving without her sweets. I couldn't believe my eyes when he stepped aside, putting the robbery on hold while we made our purchase.

This was just one example of the power Rose wielded, a power that seemed to bend reality to her will. Every morning was a battle to get her to school. She would scream and cry, refusing to go unless Dad promised he would leave work early to pick her up. This often resulted in Dad making a 60-mile round trip, a sacrifice that took a toll on his own well-being and career.

Bedtime was another battleground. Rose would only settle if Dad sat on the floor beside her bed until she fell asleep. As we shared a room, I was held hostage to her nightly rituals, unable to drift off myself until she was satisfied.

In the midst of this chaos, I found myself taking on the role of the "good" child. I was the one who went to church with Mum and Dad every Sunday, smiling through the services even when I wanted to be anywhere else. I was the one who never wanted to burden my parents with my own troubles and who tried to maintain the illusion of a happy family. But this role came at a cost. I learned to suppress my own feelings to put the needs of others before my own. This habit followed me into adulthood, impacting my ability to form healthy relationships and assert my own boundaries.

At school, I struggled to focus. The constant stress and trauma at home left little room for academic pursuits. It wasn't until years later, in a session with a clinical psychologist, that I gained some insight into my struggles. "Would you pass an exam," he asked me, "if you had a gun held to your head?" That's what it felt like growing up with Rose - a constant threat, a relentless pressure that left me in a state of survival mode.

Rose was a master manipulator, able to twist any situation to her advantage. She played the victim with finesse, leaving a trail of people eager to please her in her wake. When conflicts arose between us, she often painted me as the aggressor.

One particularly vivid memory was during our teenage years. We were getting ready to go out, a process complicated by the fact that we shared a bathroom. I was taking longer than Rose liked, and her impatience grew into rage. When I finally opened the door, she grabbed me by the hair and yanked me out. Instinctively, I pushed her away, causing her to stumble into the radiator and cut her leg. Mum and Dad were furious with me, and I was left so upset that I didn't go out at all that evening.

This was a pattern that would repeat itself over the years. Rose would prod and provoke me until I finally exploded, giving her the reaction she craved. Afterwards, I would be left drained and distraught while she revelled in the drama she had created.

Living with someone who posed a constant threat took a toll on my mental and physical health. I was always on edge, anticipating the next outburst, the next manipulation. My body was sending me clear signals to get away, but in a family dynamic, that wasn't a simple option.

As we entered adulthood, the patterns persisted. Rose would only go to work if Mum drove her and then sat outside her workplace during her breaks. I remember one particularly bitter winter morning, standing at the bus stop on my way to my own job, struggling with my umbrella in the wind and rain. Mum and Rose drove past, tooting the horn and waving cheerfully. The contrast between their cosy car and my shivering figure at the bus stop felt like a metaphor for our lives.

Rose's contempt for me was palpable, though I could never quite understand its roots. The more she lashed out, the more I tried to compensate by being helpful at home and trying not to add to my parents' stress. They were dealing with so much already, and I didn't want to be another burden.

When I started my own family in my early twenties, I found myself increasingly isolated. My friends were focused on their careers or social lives, and I had little support. Every Tuesday, Mum and Rose would go out for a day of shopping and lunches. They would drive past my house, never once inviting me to join. The loneliness was crushing, but I poured my energy into being a super-carer for my children, determined that they would never feel the rejection I had experienced.

On the rare occasions Mum would visit or look after one of my children, I would overhear Rose, accusing her of favouritism. It was a tactic that never failed to work on

Mum, and visits would become even more infrequent. When Rose got married, it seemed like a turning point. But when her husband eventually walked out, Mum and I were left to pick up the pieces. Rose sat on the floor for months, visited daily by a psychiatric nurse, while we looked after her three children. In an effort to help her and give her a sense of purpose, I offered her a part-time receptionist position at my business. It was, in hindsight, a mistake. Rose made a mockery of me in front of my staff. She would arrive late, yawn through team meetings, and sit at her desk with her coat on, emanating misery. Customers would exchange glances but smile politely. Rose was confident that, like Mum and Dad, I would say nothing to avoid a tantrum.

It took me a long time and a lot of personal work to understand that I wasn't responsible for Rose's behaviour. I couldn't control her actions, but I could control my reaction to them. I started to set boundaries to prioritise my own mental health. It wasn't easy, and the guilt was often overwhelming, but it was necessary for my own survival.

Looking back, I see how much of my life was shaped by this dynamic. The constant stress, the suppression of my own needs, the feeling of always walking on eggshells - it all left deep scars. But I also see the strength it forged within me, the resilience and empathy it nurtured.

My journey to healing was a gradual one, marked by small steps and big realisations. I learned that it was okay to put myself first and that my feelings mattered. I learned to set boundaries and stick to them, even in the face of manipulation or guilt-tripping. I surrounded myself with supportive people who saw and valued me for who I was, not for what I could do for them.

Therapy was a crucial part of my journey. Having a safe space to process my experiences to untangle the complex web of emotions was transformative. It helped me see the patterns that had been invisible to me for so long and gave me the tools to break free from them.

I also found solace in connecting with others who had experienced similar struggles. Hearing their stories and sharing my own was a powerful reminder that I wasn't alone. We were a community of survivors, each navigating our own path to healing but united in our commitment to breaking the cycle of abuse.

Today, I stand in a place of hard-won peace. The shadows of my past still linger, but they no longer control me. I've learned to embrace my own truth, honour my own needs, and surround myself with love and light.

My journey has taught me that healing is possible, even from the deepest of wounds. It has shown me the incredible resilience of the human spirit, our capacity to not just survive but to thrive in the face of adversity. It has taught me the power of self-love, of setting boundaries, and of reaching out for help when we need it.

To anyone who finds themselves resonating with my story, who is navigating their own path through the shadows of narcissistic abuse, I want to offer you the same words of hope that were once offered to me:

You are not alone.

It is not your fault.

You are worthy of love, respect, and peace.

Your story matters.

Your healing is possible.

Keep going, even when the path is dark, and the journey feels lonely. Reach out for support, guidance, and validation. Trust your own inner voice, your own strength. You have the power within you to break free, to create a life of your own design. And know that with every step you take, you are not just healing yourself - you are lighting the way for others. Your courage, your resilience, your commitment to your own well-being - it ripples out into the world, inspiring others to do the same.

Together, we are breaking the silence around narcissistic abuse. Together, we are creating a world where love doesn't hurt, where boundaries are respected, and where every individual can thrive. So, keep shining your light. The world needs your story, your strength, your hope.

The journey to healing is not a straight line. There will be setbacks, moments of doubt, and despair. But every step forward, no matter how small, is a victory. Every boundary set, every moment of self-compassion, every reach for help - these are the building blocks of your liberation.

You are not defined by what you have endured. Your scars are not a mark of shame but a testament to your survival. You are so much more than the abuse you have suffered. You are a force of nature, a beacon of resilience, a survivor in every sense of the word.

As I look back on my own journey, I am filled with gratitude. Gratitude for the people who held out a hand when I was drowning, who believed in me when I struggled to believe in myself. Gratitude for the strength I discovered within myself, a strength I never knew I possessed. I am grateful for the opportunity to turn my pain into a purpose to use my story to help others. Because that's the thing about narcissistic abuse - it can feel so isolating, so shameful, so all-consuming. But when we share our stories, when we reach out and connect with others, we start to chip away at that isolation. We start to see that we are part of a larger tapestry, a community of survivors weaving a new narrative of hope and healing.

So to you, the one reading these words, the one who may be feeling alone, afraid, or ashamed - know that you are part of this community too. Your story, your voice, your presence - it matters. You matter. And as you navigate your own journey to healing, remember: be gentle with yourself. Recovery is not a race, and there is no finish line. It's a daily practice of choosing yourself and extending the same compassion and understanding you so freely give to others.

Some days will be harder than others. There will be moments when the old patterns feel so familiar, so seductive. In those moments, anchor yourself in your truth, in your worth, in your unbreakable spirit. Reach out to your support system, lean into your self-care practices, and trust that this, too, shall pass.

Healing is a brave choice, a radical act of self-love in a world that often tells us to put ourselves last. By choosing to prioritise your own well-being, you are not just changing your own life - you are changing the very fabric of society. You are part of a movement of change-makers, truth-tellers, and dream-weavers, each one of us committed to creating a world where love is the norm and abuse is the exception.

So, keep going. Keep leaning into the light, even when the darkness feels overwhelming. Keep believing in your own inherent worthiness, even when old doubts whisper in your ear. Keep reaching for your joy, your peace, your purpose - they are your birthright, and they are waiting for you on the other side of this journey. You are not alone, and you never will be. You are part of a family of survivors, each one of us a testament to the indomitable human spirit. Together, we rise. Together, we heal. Together, we create a world where love always wins.

So, take a deep breath. Square your shoulders. And take that next step forward, knowing that a whole community is cheering you on.

The best is yet to come, and I can't wait to witness the incredible life you will create.

Chapter 8

THE TEMPESTUOUS TANTRUMS AND THE PATH TO HEALING

"When the dark clouds come, keep going." - Charlie Mackesy's

This simple yet profound wisdom from Charlie Mackesy's "The Boy, the Mole, the Fox, and the Horse" has become a guiding light for me, a reminder that even in the darkest of times, we must keep moving forward. And dark clouds were certainly a constant presence in my life growing up with my sister Rose and her tempestuous tantrums.

Imagine, if you will, a scene of utter chaos. Screaming that pierces your eardrums, objects flying across the room, shattering against walls. Words hurled like daggers, designed to cut deep, to leave scars that no one can see. This was the reality of Rose's tantrums, a storm that would sweep through our family home, leaving devastation in its wake.

These episodes were not just unpleasant; they were deeply traumatic. The sheer intensity of Rose's rage, the viciousness of her words, would leave me feeling physically ill, my nerves frayed to the point of snapping. I would often find myself shaking, my heart pounding in my chest as if my body was preparing for a physical attack. And in a way, it was an attack. Maybe not physically, but emotionally and psychologically. Each tantrum was like a bombardment on my sense of safety, my sense of self. I never knew what would trigger Rose's rage, what innocent comment or action would be twisted into a perceived slight, a justification for her explosive anger.

Our family GP became a regular fixture in our lives, called upon to help navigate the aftermath of these storms. But no matter what he prescribed, Rose refused to take it. Medication, therapy, coping strategies - she rejected them all, leaving us to find our own ways to survive in the tumultuous environment she created. Mum bore the brunt of it, always trying to soothe, to placate, to find a way to calm the storm. I watched as she withered under the constant stress, her eyes often red from crying, her shoulders sagging under the weight of helplessness. It broke my heart to see this strong, loving woman reduced to a state of constant worry and fear.

Dad, too, suffered in his own way. He was a rock, a pillar of strength for our family, always trying to protect us from the worst of the storms. But even rocks can crumble under constant pressure. I remember one particular tantrum, one that must have been especially vicious, because I saw something I had never seen before my father crying. This man, who embodied resilience and fortitude, had been brought to tears by the unrelenting force of Rose's rage. That moment shattered something in me, a childish belief that my parents could somehow make everything okay.

As for me, I learned to make myself small and avoid drawing attention to myself lest I trigger another explosion. I became a master at reading Rose's moods and anticipating her needs and wants before she even voiced them. I thought, foolishly, that if I could just be good enough, quiet enough, helpful enough, I could somehow prevent the tantrums. But, of course, that was an illusion. Nothing I did or didn't do could control Rose's behaviour. Her tantrums were like forces of nature, unpredictable and unstoppable. And as much as I tried to tell myself that it wasn't personal, that her anger wasn't really directed at me, it was hard not to internalise the venom she spewed.

Slowly, insidiously, my love for my sister began to erode under the constant barrage of her cruelty. I found myself resenting her, even hating her at times. Guilt would quickly follow these feelings - after all, she was my sister, and I was supposed to love her unconditionally. But how do you love someone who seems determined to hurt you?

It wasn't until many years later, after a life-altering event of my own, that I began to gain some perspective on my childhood experiences. A brain haemorrhage, a brush with death, and the subsequent need for trauma counselling led me to a clinical psychologist who would change my life.

In those early sessions, I was a mess. The trauma of my medical emergency had cracked open the vault of my childhood memories, and all the pain, fear, and confusion came pouring out. I talked about Rose, about the tantrums, about the constant feeling of walking on eggshells. For the first time, I had someone who really listened, validated my experiences, and helped me see that I wasn't crazy and that what I had endured was not normal or okay.

My psychologist helped me understand that Rose's behaviour was likely rooted in her own struggles, her own unmet needs, and unresolved traumas. This didn't excuse her actions, but it did help me start to separate her behaviour from my own sense of self-worth. I began to see that her tantrums, as terrifying and hurtful as they were, were not about me. They were manifestations of her own inner turmoil, her own inability to regulate her emotions.

This understanding was a turning point for me. It didn't erase the scars of my childhood, but it did start to lessen their hold over me. I began to learn about boundaries, self-care, and the importance of prioritising my own mental health. I learned that it was okay to love my sister while also recognising that her behaviour was toxic and that I needed to protect myself from it.

Healing, I discovered, was not a linear process. There were days when the old fears and resentments would resurface, days when a loud noise or an angry voice would trigger a panic response. However, with the tools I was learning in therapy and the support of my psychologist and loved ones, I was able to navigate these setbacks with increasing resilience.

A key part of my healing journey was learning to reframe my narrative. For so long, I had seen myself as a victim, powerless in the face of Rose's tantrums. But my psychologist helped me see the strength in my story, the resilience I had shown in surviving such a tumultuous upbringing. I began to see myself not as a victim but as a survivor, someone who had faced incredible adversity and come out the other side.

This shift in perspective was empowering. It allowed me to start reclaiming my story, to see the ways in which I had coped and adapted, the ways in which I had found small moments of joy and connection even in the midst of chaos. It helped me start to let go of the shame and self-blame I had carried for so long. Of course, the scars of those years can never be fully erased. They are part of my story, part of what has shaped me into the person I am today. But I've learned that these scars do not define me. I am so much more than the sum of my traumas.

My journey of healing has been a process of learning to love and trust myself again, of rebuilding the sense of safety and self-worth that was so eroded by those tumultuous years. It has been a journey of learning to set boundaries, to advocate for my own needs, and to surround myself with people who uplift and support me. It has also been a journey of learning to extend compassion - to myself, for the child I was and the adult I am, navigating this path as best I can, and even to Rose, who I've come to see as someone who was also deeply hurt, someone who never learned healthy ways to cope with her own pain.

This compassion doesn't mean accepting or excusing abusive behaviour. It doesn't mean putting myself in harm's way or tolerating mistreatment. But it does mean recognising the humanity in everyone, the ways in which we are all products of our experiences, all fighting our own unseen battles.

Today, I can look back on those dark years with a sense of distance, even a sense of gratitude. Not for the pain and trauma itself, but for the strength and resilience it forged in me, for the empathy and insight it has given me, for the appreciation it has instilled in me for the peace and stability I have worked so hard to create in my life.

To anyone reading this who may have experienced similar traumas, whether from a sibling, a parent, or anyone else, I want to say this: your experiences are valid. Your pain is real. And you are not alone. The path to healing is not always straightforward, and it looks different for everyone. But know that healing is possible. Know that you have incredible strength within you, even if you can't always feel it. Know that you deserve peace, safety, and love and that there are people and resources out there to help you find them. Keep going, even when the dark clouds come. Keep reaching out, keep telling your story, and keep believing in your own worth and resilience. You are so much stronger than you know.

And to my younger self, the little girl who hid in her room, who tried so hard to be invisible, who carried so much fear and pain - I see you. I honour you. And I thank you for your strength, your courage, and your unwavering ability to keep going, even in the darkest of times. You are the reason I am here today, the reason I can tell this story, the reason I can extend hope and empathy to others.

We survived little one. We survived, and we are learning to thrive. The tantrums no longer control us. We are writing our own story now, and it is a story of healing, of resilience, of hope.

So, to all of you reading this, whether you are in the thick of the storm or navigating the aftermath, know that you are not alone. Know that your story matters. Know that there is always hope, even in the darkest of times. Keep going. Keep shining your light. The world needs your strength, your compassion, and your unbridled resilience.

Together, we can weather any storm.

Chapter 9

BREAKING FREE AND FINDING YOUR VOICE

"You must be the change you wish to see in the world." - Mahatma Gandhi

These profound words from Mahatma Gandhi have been a guiding light for me on my journey of breaking free from the chains of narcissistic abuse and finding my own voice. They serve as a reminder that the power to transform our lives lies within us and that we have the ability to shape our own narratives and create the change we wish to see.

For so long, I lived my life on autopilot, rushing from one task to the next, barely pausing to catch my breath. It was a coping mechanism, I realise now, a way to avoid confronting the painful reality of my relationship with my sister Rose. If I kept myself busy enough, I didn't have to think about the constant demands, the emotional manipulation, the toxic patterns that had become so ingrained in our dynamic. But then, a health crisis forced me to stop. Literally, facing the prospect of major surgery, I found myself with an abundance of something I hadn't had in years: time. Time to rest, to reflect, to really examine the life I had been living and the relationships that shaped it.

In that stillness, I began to notice things I had been too busy to see before. I noticed how, even in the midst of my health struggles, Rose continued to seek me out, to make requests and demands of my time and energy. I noticed the familiar tug of obligation, the knee-jerk response to put her needs before my own, even as I lay in a hospital bed. But this time, something was different. As I lay there, recovering from surgery, I felt a stirring of emotions I had long suppressed. Anger at the realisation that even now, in my most vulnerable state, I was expected to cater to Rose's whims. Sadness for the years I had spent contorting myself to fit her needs at the expense of my own. And grief, a deep, aching grief, for the relationship we could have had if not for the toxicity that had tainted it.

These emotions, painful as they were, were also a gift. They were a wake-up call, a signpost pointing me towards a truth I had long avoided: that the patterns in my relationship with Rose were not healthy and that I deserved better.

The main gain in recognising these painful patterns is that we can then reduce or try to reduce our participation in them. For me, this meant learning to pause before automatically responding to Rose's requests. It meant checking in with myself, asking: Is this reasonable? How am I feeling? Do I have the emotional reserve to manage this? And, most importantly, do I want to respond at all?

These were revolutionary questions for me. For so long, I had operated on the assumption that I had to respond, that I had to meet every demand placed on me, no matter the cost to my own well-being. The idea that I had a choice, that I could prioritise my own needs, was foreign and frightening. But I knew I had to start somewhere. So, I began small, with simple acts of self-assertion. Letting a call from Rose go to voicemail when I was feeling particularly drained. Saying no to a request that would have required me to cancel my own plans. These small acts of the resistance felt monumental, each one a tiny reclamation of my own agency.

As I continued on this path, I came to a painful but liberating realisation: people with narcissistic personalities rarely change. No matter how much I might wish for a different relationship with Rose, the reality was that she was unlikely to suddenly develop empathy to start considering my needs as equal to her own.

This realisation was a turning point for me. It meant that if I wanted to change, I had to be the one to initiate it. I had to be the one to set boundaries to communicate my needs clearly and firmly, even if they fell on deaf ears. Sometimes, stating our needs is enough. There were moments when I was able to have frank conversations with Rose to express how her actions were impacting me. But more often than not, I found myself up against a wall of defensiveness, of denial, of outright hostility.

In those moments, I learned the power of silence. Of allowing my lack of response to speak volumes. It was a hard lesson, going against every instinct I had to placate to smooth things over. But I came to understand that not responding is a valid response, especially when our words are falling on deaf ears.

This shift in approach brought up a lot of guilt for me. Guilt for not being the ever-accommodating sister I had always been, for not dropping everything to meet Rose's needs. But with the help of therapy and a lot of self-reflection, I began to understand that this guilt was not mine to carry.

The guilt we feel about not meeting others' requests is not ours; it is our pattern of taking responsibility, compensating, and tidying up a mess that was never ours. Recognising these patterns can be very painful, but living unaware of their impact is much more damaging.

As I started to shed this misplaced guilt, I found myself stepping into a new sense of empowerment. I began to see that I had a right to my own time, my own space, and my own emotional energy. That I was not obligated to set myself on fire to keep someone else warm.

This newfound sense of empowerment spilt over into other areas of my life. I found myself speaking up more at work and setting healthier boundries in my friendships. It was as if, by learning to stand up to Rose, I had unlocked a reservoir of inner strength I never knew I had. Of course, this journey was not without its challenges. There were times when the old patterns would resurface when I would find myself slipping back into the role of the accommodating, self-sacrificing sister. There were moments of doubt, of questioning whether I was being selfish or unreasonable in my newfound assertiveness.

But each time, I would remind myself of how far I had come. I would think back to those painful realisations in the hospital, the grief and anger that had propelled me onto this path of self-discovery. And I would reaffirm my commitment to my own well-being to creating a life that was authentic and fulfilling on my own terms. Through this process, I discovered the transformative power of finding my own voice and learning to express my needs, my boundaries, and my truth, even when it was difficult or uncomfortable. I learned that my voice matters, that I matter, regardless of how anyone else might respond.

This is the message I want to impart to anyone else navigating the rocky terrain of narcissistic abuse: your voice matters. Your needs matter. You matter inherently and unconditionally, regardless of how well you meet anyone else's expectations.

Breaking free from the patterns of narcissistic abuse is not easy. It requires a willingness to confront painful truths, to sit with uncomfortable emotions, to risk the disapproval or even the wrath of those who have long controlled us. But freedom, on the other hand, is worth every difficult step.

Reclaiming your power, your voice, your life - it's a journey of a thousand tiny revolutions. It's in every boundary set, every "no" uttered, every moment of self-care and self-compassion. It's in the gradual untangling of your own wants and needs from the demands and expectations of others. And it's a journey that looks different for everyone. There is no one-size-fits-all approach to healing from narcissistic abuse, no magic formula for breaking free. What matters is that you are taking steps, however small, towards a life that feels authentic and nurturing to you.

For some, this may mean a complete cessation of contact with the narcissistic individual. For others, it may involve a radical restructuring of the relationship, with firm boundaries and limited engagement. For some, it may be an ongoing process of negotiation, of give and take, of learning to assert oneself while still maintaining some form of connection. Whatever your path looks like, know that you are not alone. There is a vast community of survivors out there, each navigating their own journey of healing and empowerment. Reach out, share your story, and lean on the support and wisdom of those who have walked this path before you.

And above all, be gentle with yourself. Breaking free from narcissistic abuse is a process, not an event. There will be setbacks, moments of self-doubt, and times when you fall back into old patterns. This is normal, and it does not negate your progress.

Remember, you are unlearning years, often decades, of conditioning. You are rewiring your brain, rewriting your story, reclaiming your identity. This takes time, patience, and immense self-compassion.

Celebrate every victory, no matter how small. Every time you speak your truth, every time you prioritise your own needs, every time you show yourself the kindness and understanding you have so long extended to others - these are monumental achievements. These are the building blocks of your liberation.

As you continue on this journey, keep Mahatma Gandhi's words close to your heart. "You must be the change you wish to see in the world." By breaking free from the cycles of narcissistic abuse by reclaiming your power and your voice, you are not only changing your own world - you are contributing to a global shift towards healthier, more compassionate ways of being.

Your story, your healing, your triumph - it matters. It matters not just for you but for every person who will be touched by the ripple effects of your transformation. Every boundary you set, every act of self-love you practice, every truth you speak - these are not just personal victories. They are acts of revolution, of reclamation, of profound social change.

So keep going, even when the path is steep, and the terrain is rough. Keep speaking your truth, even when your voice shakes. Keep believing in your own inherent worth, even when others try to diminish it. You are the change. You are the revolution. You are the voice that will not be silenced. And with every step you take, you are not just reclaiming your own life - you are lighting the way for others. You are proof that healing is possible, that there is life after narcissistic abuse, and that even the deepest scars can be transformed into sources of strength and resilience.

Keep shining your light. The world needs your story, your courage, your unbreakable spirit.

You've got this. And you are never, ever alone.

Chapter 10

UNMASKING THE NARCISSIST: RECOGNISING THE RED FLAGS

"Some cause happiness wherever they go; others whenever they go." - Oscar Wilde

This witty observation, Oscar Wilde, encapsulates the profound impact that different personalities can have on our lives. When it comes to narcissistic individuals, their presence often brings a trail of confusion, hurt, and emotional turmoil. Learning to recognise the red flags of narcissistic behaviour is a crucial step in protecting ourselves and navigating these complex relationships.

In my journey of healing from narcissistic abuse, I've become all too familiar with the traits that characterise this personality disorder. It's a knowledge born from painful experience, from countless instances of being lied to, gaslit, and emotionally exploited. But it's also a knowledge that has empowered me, allowing me to spot the warning signs and establish healthier boundaries.

One of the most striking traits of narcissists is their propensity for lying. It's not just the occasional white lie or embellishment – narcissists lie effortlessly and frequently. They'll lie about their accomplishments, their relationships, and even their own feelings and intentions. I remember catching Rose in countless lies over the years, from small fibs about where she was going to grand tales of her own importance. At first, I would confront her attempt to understand why she felt the need to deceive. But I quickly learned that a narcissist's lies are not about the truth – they're about control, about maintaining the carefully crafted image they present to the world.

Closely tied to this pattern of deceit is a notable absence of genuine apologies. Narcissists rarely apologise, and when they do, it's often with an ulterior motive. They might offer a superficial "I'm sorry" to get out of trouble or to manipulate you into forgiving them. But a true apology, one that acknowledges the hurt caused and takes responsibility for their actions? That's a rarity. I can count on one hand the number of times Rose genuinely apologised to me, and even then, it was usually followed by a justification or a deflection of blame.

Another red flag that took me years to recognise was the constant undercurrent of envy in my interactions with Rose. Narcissists are often deeply envious of others, whether it's their possessions, their relationships, or their successes. But rather than admire or celebrate others' achievements, they seek to undermine them. I remember the snide comments Rose would make about my friendships and the way she would belittle my accomplishments at work. At the time, I internalised these comments, wondering if perhaps I wasn't as successful or likeable as I thought. It was only later that I understood this behaviour for what it was: a reflection of her own insecurities and need to feel superior.

Perhaps one of the most insidious traits of narcissists is their use of gaslighting. Gaslighting is a form of psychological manipulation in which the abuser seeks to sow seeds of doubt in the victim's mind, making them question their own memory, perception, and sanity. It's a tactic I know all too well. Rose would often rewrite the narrative of our interactions, denying things she had said or done or twisting my words to make me doubt my own recollection. The result was a constant state of confusion and self-doubt, a feeling that I couldn't trust my own mind.

Narcissists are also very particular about the company they keep. They surround themselves with individuals who serve their needs and reinforce their sense of self-importance. These relationships are not about genuine connection – they're about utility. I watched as Rose cycled through friends and partners, each one selected for what they could offer her, whether it was admiration, financial support, or social status. When they no longer served her needs, she would discard them without a second thought.

In her interactions with me, Rose had a knack for making me feel unimportant, even worthless. It was a slow erosion of my self-esteem, a gradual chipping away at my sense of self. She would dismiss my opinions, ignore my needs, and constantly prioritise her own wants and feelings. If I tried to assert myself, I was met with defensiveness and hostility. It took me a long time to understand that this wasn't about me – it was about her need for control and superiority.

This defensiveness is another common trait of narcissists. They have a fragile sense of self that is easily threatened by any perceived criticism or challenge to their authority. I learned to walk on eggshells around Rose, carefully choosing my words to avoid triggering her anger. But even the most innocuous comments could be twisted and turned against me. It was an exhausting dance, one that left me feeling constantly on edge.

Perhaps most troubling of all is the way narcissists exploit others without guilt. They view people as objects to be used for their own gain, whether it's emotionally, financially, or otherwise. I experienced this firsthand when I offered Rose a job at my company. What I intended as a gesture of support quickly turned into an opportunity for her to undermine me professionally. She would show up late, neglect her duties, and even speak badly of me to my employees. When I confronted her, she showed no remorse, no acknowledgement of the impact her behaviour had on me and my business.

This sense of entitlement is a hallmark of narcissistic behaviour. Narcissists believe they are owed special treatment, and the rules don't apply to them. They expect others to cater to their needs and desires, regardless of the cost. For Rose, this manifested in constant demands on my time and energy, an expectation that I would drop everything to attend to her wants. When these entitled expectations aren't met, narcissists often resort to bullying and put-downs. It's a tactic designed to keep others in line to maintain their sense of superiority. Rose was a master at this, knowing just what buttons to push to make me feel small and inadequate. She would criticise my appearance, mock my dreams and goals, and constantly compare me unfavourably to herself or others.

Recognising these traits was a process of years for me, a gradual awakening to the unhealthy dynamics at play in my relationship with Rose. It was a painful realisation, one that forced me to confront some hard truths about my own role in enabling and tolerating her behaviour. But it was also an empowering realisation, one that allowed me to start setting boundaries and prioritising my own well-being.

If you find yourself resonating with these experiences, know that you are not alone. Narcissistic abuse is a complex and often invisible form of trauma, one that can leave deep scars on our psyche and our sense of self. But healing is possible. Recognising the red flags is the first step, but it's also important to seek support, whether through therapy, support groups, or trusted loved ones.

It's crucial to remember that a narcissist's behaviour is not about you. It's not a reflection of your worth or your lovability. Narcissists act out of their own deep-seated insecurities and need for control. Recognising this can help to alleviate some of the self-blame and shame that often accompanies these relationships.

As you navigate this journey of healing, be gentle with yourself. Untangling yourself from a narcissistic relationship is a process, one that requires patience, self-compassion, and a commitment to your own well-being. There will be setbacks and challenges along the way. You may find yourself falling back into old patterns of self-doubt or accommodating behaviour. This is normal, and it doesn't negate your progress. Keep in mind that setting boundaries with a narcissist can be challenging. They may respond with anger, manipulation, or attempts to undermine your resolve. This is where a strong support system and a solid sense of self come into play. Surround yourself with people who affirm your worth and your right to healthy relationships.

It's also important to focus on rebuilding your own sense of self. Narcissistic abuse can erode our self-esteem, leaving us questioning our own judgment and intuition.

Take time to reconnect with your values, your passions, and your goals. Engage in activities that bring you joy and fulfilment, independent of others' opinions or validation.

As you continue on this path of healing, remember that your story and your experiences matter. Sharing your journey can be a powerful way to reclaim your narrative and connect with others who have faced similar struggles. You never know who you might inspire or whose life you might change by speaking your truth. And always remember, you are worthy of love, respect, and healthy relationships. You have the right to set boundaries, prioritise your own needs, and walk away from situations that diminish or exploit you. Your healing is a testament to your strength, your resilience, and your unbreakable spirit.

In the words of Oscar Wilde, *"To love oneself is the beginning of a lifelong romance."* May your journey of healing be a love story to yourself, a rekindling of the inherent worth and beauty that has always resided within you. You deserve nothing less. Keep going. Keep unmasking the narcissists in your life, keep setting those boundaries, and keep choosing yourself. The world needs your light, your truth, and your unbreakable spirit.

You've got this. And you are never, ever alone.

Chapter 11

MY JOURNEY OF SELF-DISCOVERY AND RESILIENCE

"To live a good life: we have the potential for it if we learn to be indifferent to what makes no difference." - Marcus Aurelius

These profound words from Marcus Aurelius have become a guiding light in my journey of healing from narcissistic abuse. They remind me that I have the power to choose what I focus on, to direct my energy toward what truly matters, and to let go of the rest.

In the aftermath of my experiences with Rose, I found myself on a path of self-discovery, learning to prioritise my own well-being and build a life that was authentic and fulfilling. It hasn't been an easy journey, but through trial and error, I've discovered several strategies that have been instrumental in my healing process.

One of the most crucial steps for me was learning to create and maintain healthy boundaries. For so long, I had allowed Rose's needs and wants to take precedence over my own, sacrificing my time, energy, and emotional well-being in the process. Establishing boundaries was a way of reclaiming my autonomy and communicating that my needs mattered, too.

At first, setting boundaries felt foreign and uncomfortable. I was so used to being available at Rose's beck and call that the idea of saying "no" or putting my own needs first felt selfish. But with practice, I began to see the power in this simple act. Each boundary I set was a declaration of my self-worth, a message to myself and others that I deserved respect and consideration.

Creating boundaries looked different in different situations. Sometimes, it was as simple as not answering the phone when I needed some quiet time to recharge. Other times, it involved having difficult conversations expressing my limits and expectations clearly and firmly. It wasn't always easy, and I often faced pushback or manipulation from Rose. However, I learned that the temporary discomfort of enforcing a boundary was far more preferable than the long-term pain of having my boundaries consistently violated.

Another strategy that has been invaluable in my healing journey is the practice of taking micro-breaks. In the thick of Rose's demands and dramas, I often felt like I was drowning, unable to catch my breath. Taking small breaks, even just an hour or two of switching off my phone and focusing on my own needs, was like coming up for air.

These micro-breaks became sacred spaces for me, moments where I could reconnect with myself and my own desires. Sometimes, I would use this time to engage in a hobby or activity that brought me joy, like reading a book or tending to my garden. Other times, I would sit in silence, allowing myself to feel my emotions without judgment or expectation.

I found that the more I practised these moments of self-care, the more resilient I became in the face of Rose's narcissistic behaviour. It was as if by nurturing myself, I was building up an inner reserve of strength and clarity that could weather any storm.

A key aspect of this self-care was learning to stay calm and practice self-compassion. Dealing with a narcissist can be incredibly triggering, and I often find myself getting swept up in waves of anger, frustration and hurt. In these moments, it was crucial for me to remember to be gentle with myself and acknowledge my feelings without getting lost in them.

One tool that was particularly helpful in cultivating this sense of calm was yoga. I had always been sceptical of yoga, associating it with impossible postures and new-age spirituality. But when a friend dragged me to a class, I was surprised to find a profound sense of peace and presence on the mat.

In yoga, I learned to focus on my breath to be aware of my body and my thoughts without getting attached to them. It became a practice of letting go, of releasing the tension and stress that I carried with me. I found that in the midst of a challenging pose or a difficult emotion, I could always come back to my breath, to that unchanging centre of calm within me. Yoga also taught me the importance of being aware of my own needs. In a narcissistic relationship, it's easy to lose sight of what we need and want to become so focused on pleasing the other person that we forget to take care of ourselves. On the mat, I learned to listen to my body, honour its limits, and respect its desires. This was a skill that I began to carry off the mat and into my daily life.

Of course, there were times when no amount of boundary-setting or self-care could shield me from Rose's toxic behaviour. In these instances, I learned the importance of avoidance. I realised that I would never win an argument with a narcissist and that engaging in their twisted logic and manipulation was a losing game. Instead, I learned to create distance, to remove myself from the situation when possible.

This wasn't always easy, especially given the familial ties that bound me to Rose. But I learned to be strategic in my interactions, to limit my exposure to her toxicity. I would keep our conversations brief and focused, avoiding any topics that I knew would trigger her narcissistic rage. If a conversation started to escalate, I would calmly excuse myself, refusing to be drawn into her drama.

A crucial part of this process was educating myself about narcissistic personality disorder. The more I learned about the traits and tactics of narcissists, the more I was able to recognise the patterns in Rose's behaviour. This knowledge was empowering, helping me to trust my own perceptions and not get lost in self-doubt.

I devoured books, articles, and online resources about narcissistic abuse. I connected with others who had experienced similar relationships, finding solace and validation in their stories. Slowly but surely, I began to piece together a narrative that made sense, one that acknowledged the reality of what I had experienced and affirmed that it wasn't my fault. This education was particularly important when it came to the gaslighting that is so common in narcissistic relationships. Rose was a master at making me question my own reality, at twisting my words and memories until I didn't know what to believe. By learning about gaslighting tactics, I was able to start catching her in the act to hold onto my truth even in the face of her manipulations.

But perhaps the hardest lesson I've had to learn is knowing when to leave a relationship. For years, I clung to the hope that Rose would change, that if I just loved her enough and supported her enough, I could help her heal from her own wounds. But I've come to understand that this was a false hope, one that kept me trapped in a cycle of abuse.

Narcissists rarely change, not because they can't, but because they don't see a need to. Their behaviour serves them and allows them to maintain their sense of superiority and control. Waiting for a narcissist to change is like waiting for a mirage in the desert – the closer you get, the more it dissolves into nothingness.

Leaving a relationship, especially a familial one, is never easy. It's a decision that comes with a great deal of grief, guilt, and fear. But I've learned that sometimes, it's the only way to save ourselves. It's an act of radical self-love, of choosing our own well-being over the comfort of the familiar.

In my journey of healing, I've found that one of the most important resources is a strong support system. Surrounding myself with a core group of friends and family who understand what I've been through and who remind me of my worth and strengths has been invaluable. These relationships have been an emotional buffer, a safe haven where I can be seen and heard without judgment.

Building this support system has required vulnerability and the willingness to share my story and ask for help. It's not always been comfortable, and I've had to navigate the fear of being a burden or of not being believed.

But I've found that the more I've opened up, the more I've discovered that I'm not alone and that there are so many others who have faced similar struggles.

In addition to my human support system, I've also found great solace in the natural world. There's something about being in nature that calms my mind and soothes my soul. Whether it's taking my dogs for a long walk in the woods or getting my hands dirty in the garden, immersing myself in the beauty and simplicity of the outdoors has been a balm for my wounded spirit.

Nature has a way of putting things in perspective, of reminding me that there is a world beyond my own struggles and pains. In the face of a majestic mountain or a delicate flower, my problems seem to shrink, not disappearing but becoming more manageable. It's in nature that I feel most connected to something greater than myself, most able to tap into a well of resilience and peace.

Another tool that has been crucial in my healing journey is meditation. Like yoga, meditation was something I initially resisted, associating it with an unattainable state of blissful enlightenment. But as I've developed my practice, I've come to understand meditation as simply a way of being present, of observing my thoughts and emotions without getting caught up in them.

In the quiet space of meditation, I've learned to witness my own inner landscape without judgment. I've seen how my mind can be both my greatest ally and my greatest enemy, capable of spinning stories of despair or weaving visions of hope. Meditation has taught me that I have a choice in which stories I feed and which thoughts I allow to take root and grow.

Perhaps most importantly, meditation has helped me cultivate a sense of inner peace and stability that is not dependent on external circumstances. In the midst of chaos and conflict, I've learned that I can always find a stillness within, a place of calm abiding that is untouched by the storms of life. This has been an incredible source of strength and resilience, a reminder that I have the tools to weather any challenge.

Finally, one of the most joyful discoveries in my healing journey has been the power of hobbies and service. For so long, my life revolved around Rose and her dramas, leaving little room for my own interests and passions. As I've created more distance and boundaries, I've had the space to rediscover the things that bring me alive.

One of these has been volunteering for a local charity that supports survivors of domestic violence. Being able to turn my own pain into a source of support and empowerment for others has been incredibly healing. It's allowed me to find meaning and purpose in my experiences, to transform my struggle into a gift of service.

I've also rekindled my love for painting, a hobby I had abandoned years ago. In the flow of colour and form, I lose myself in a world of beauty and creation. It's a reminder that I am not just a survivor but a creator, capable of bringing new life and joy into being.

As I reflect on my journey, I'm struck by how far I've come. The path of healing from narcissistic abuse is not a straight line but a winding road with many detours and setbacks. There have been times of great darkness when I didn't know if I had the strength to keep going. But I've learned that healing is not a destination but a practice, a daily choice to show up for myself with compassion and care. I've also learned that I am so much more than what I have endured. My experiences with Rose have shaped me, but they do not define me. I am a work in progress, always learning, always growing, always becoming more fully myself.

To anyone else on this path, I want to offer these words of hope and encouragement: You are not alone. What you have experienced is real, and it matters. Your pain is valid, and so is your healing.

Healing is possible, even when it feels like an impossible dream. It's in the small, daily choices – the boundaries set, the moments of self-care, the reach for support. It's in the decision to keep going, to believe in your own resilience and worth.

Your story is still being written, and you are the author. You have the power to shape the narrative to choose the themes of healing and hope. You have the right to create a life of joy, peace, and fulfilment.

So, keep going, my friend. Keep learning, keep growing, keep choosing yourself. The journey is not always easy, but it is always, always worth it. And remember, even in the darkest of times, you carry a light within you that can never be extinguished. Let that light guide you, sustain you, and remind you of the unbreakable beauty of your spirit.

You've got this. And you are so deeply loved.

CONCLUSION

"The best revenge is not to be like your enemy." - Marcus Aurelius

---

As I come to the end of this journey of sharing my story and the lessons I've learned along the way, these words from Marcus Aurelius echo in my mind. They serve as a powerful reminder that the true path to healing, to liberation, is not about retribution or spite but about reclaiming our own lives and our own sense of self.

Narcissistic abuse is a complex and insidious beast, one that can leave deep, invisible scars on our psyche and soul. It can make us question our own reality, doubt our own worth, and feel trapped in a never-ending cycle of pain and confusion. But as I hope my story has shown, healing is possible. Freedom is possible. A life of joy, peace, and self-love is possible.

The journey of healing is not a straight line. It's a winding path, full of ups and downs, forwards and backwards. There will be days when the old patterns and fears resurface when the voice of the narcissist seems louder than your own inner wisdom. In those moments, remember to be kind to yourself. Remember that healing is not about perfection but about progress, about the daily choice to show up for yourself with compassion and patience.

One of the best pieces of advice I received in my own journey was to imagine a radio playing in the background. The noise might be constant, even overwhelming at times. But you have the power to turn down the volume and focus your attention elsewhere.

This imagery has been so helpful for me in dealing with the lingering effects of narcissistic abuse. When the old doubts and anxieties start to creep in, when I find myself replaying past hurts or fearing future manipulations, I imagine myself turning down the volume. I redirect my focus to the present moment, to the things and people that bring me joy and peace.

It's a practice, a muscle that grows stronger with use. And as you flex this muscle of redirection, of choosing where to place your attention, you'll find that the hold of the narcissist begins to loosen. You'll start to reclaim your mental and emotional space, to create room for your own thoughts, your own desires, your own truth.

And your truth, my friend, is this: You are worthy. You are lovable. You are enough, exactly as you are. The narcissist's behaviour, words, and actions arc not a reflection of your value or your worth. They are a reflection of their own deep-seated wounds, their own unhealed pain.

As you continue on this path of healing, hold onto this truth like a lifeline. Let it be your anchor in the stormy seas, your compass when you feel lost in the fog. Let it guide you back to yourself, to the unbreakable light that shines within you.

Surround yourself with people and practices that remind you of this truth. Build a support system of friends, family, therapists, and fellow survivors who see your worth, validate your experiences, and cheer you on as you reclaim your life. Engage in activities that bring you joy and help you reconnect with your own passions and desires. Create rituals of self-care and self-compassion, daily reminders that you deserve love and kindness from others and yourself.

As you do this work, remember that you are not just healing yourself - you are breaking a cycle of abuse that may have spanned generations. By choosing to face your pain, work through your trauma, and rewrite your story, you are not only liberating yourself, but you are also paving the way for others. Your courage, your resilience, your commitment to your own healing - these are powerful forces of change in the world.

So, as you step into this new chapter of your life, know that you do not walk alone. You are part of a community of survivors, each on their own journey of healing, each a testament to the indomitable strength of the human spirit. Draw strength from their stories, and know that your own story will be a source of light for someone else.

The path ahead may not always be easy, but it is filled with possibility. Every day, you have the opportunity to choose healing, to choose growth, to choose yourself. Every day, you have the chance to write a new story to create a life that is authentic, joyful, and free.

As you turn the page on this chapter of your life, I invite you to embrace the unknown and to lean into the discomfort of growth and change. Trust in your own strength, your own wisdom, your own unbreakable spirit. You have survived so much, and you have the power within you to thrive.

Remember, healing is not about becoming who you were before the abuse. It's about discovering who you can be in the aftermath, who you are when you are free to be fully and unapologetically yourself. It's about falling in love with this version of yourself, scars and all.

So, here's to you, survivor. Here's to your courage, your resilience, your boundless capacity for love and healing. Here's to the beautiful life that awaits you, the life you so deeply deserve.

Keep turning down the volume on the noise that no longer serves you. Keep turning up the volume on your own truth, your own desires, and your own beautiful dreams. Keep choosing yourself every single day. And always remember: You are not alone. You are believed. You are loved.

Here's to the next chapter of your story. I can't wait to see the magnificent places it takes you.

With all my love and belief in you,

A fellow survivor on the path to healing.